A Rocket
in My Pocket

A Rocket in My Pocket

THE RHYMES AND CHANTS OF YOUNG AMERICANS

COMPILED BY CARL WITHERS

ILLUSTRATED BY SUSANNE SUBA

Henry Holt and Company • New York

Copyright © 1948 by Carl Withers
All rights reserved, including the right to reproduce
this book or portions thereof in any form.
Published by Henry Holt and Company, Inc.,
115 West 18th Street, New York, New York 10011.
Published in Canada by Fitzhenry & Whiteside Limited,
195 Allstate Parkway, Markham, Ontario L3R 4T8.

Library of Congress Cataloging-in-Publication Data is available.
Library of Congress Catalog Card Number: 48-4881

ISBN 0-8050-0821-7 (hardcover)
ISBN 0-8050-0804-7 (paperback)

10 9 8 7 6 5 4 3 2 1

First published in hardcover by Henry Holt and Company, Inc., in 1948.
Reissued in hardcover in 1988.
First Owlet edition—1988

Printed in the United States of America

ISBN 0-8050-0821-7 HARDCOVER
ISBN 0-8050-0804-7 PAPERBACK

C O N T E N T S

```
C   O   N   T   E   N   T   S
h   n   u   e   a   e   e   t
r   u   t   n   t   v   a   i
i   t   s       t   e   c   n
s   s           t   r   h   g
t                       e   y
m                       r
a                       s
s
```

Read the words from right to left

[v]

PREFACE

Peter
Rabbit
Eats
Fish
And
Catches
Eels.

Read initial letters down

Eels
Catch
Alligators;
Father
Eats
Raw
Potaters.

Read initial letters up

Silence in the courtroom!
The monkey wants to speak.

Rhymes for Fun

I scream, you scream,
We all scream for ice cream.

*

I says, you says,
We all want ices.

*

My boy friend's name is Jello;
He comes from Monticello,
With a pimple on his nose
And two flat toes.
And that's the way my story goes.

*

Far over the hills, a good way off,
A donkey caught the whooping cough.

[3]

Chick, chick, chatterman
How much are your geese?
Chick, chick, chatterman
Five cents apiece.
Chick, chick, chatterman
That's too dear.
Chick, chick, chatterman
Get out of here.

*

Monkey, monkey, sittin' on a rail,
Pickin' his teeth with the end of his tail.

*

A big bumblebee
Sat on a wall;
He said he could hum
And that was all.

[4]

Way down South where bananas grow,
A grasshopper stepped on an elephant's toe.
The elephant said, with tears in his eyes,
"Pick on somebody your own size."

Old Lady Fry
Wore heels a mile high,
And when she walked by me
I thought I would die.

Oh, the funniest thing I've ever seen
Was a tomcat sewing on a sewing machine.
Oh, the sewing machine got running too slow,
And it took seven stitches in the tomcat's toe.

[7]

Did you ever ever ever
In your life, did you ever
See a whale catch a snail by the tail?
No, I never never never
In my life, no I never
Saw a whale catch a snail by the tail.

＊

I asked my mother for fifty cents
To see the elephant jump the fence.
He jumped so high he reached the sky,
And didn't get back till the Fourth of July.

＊

I asked my mother for fifty cents,
I asked my father for fifty more;
He grabbed me by the seat of the pants
And pushed me out the door.

[8]

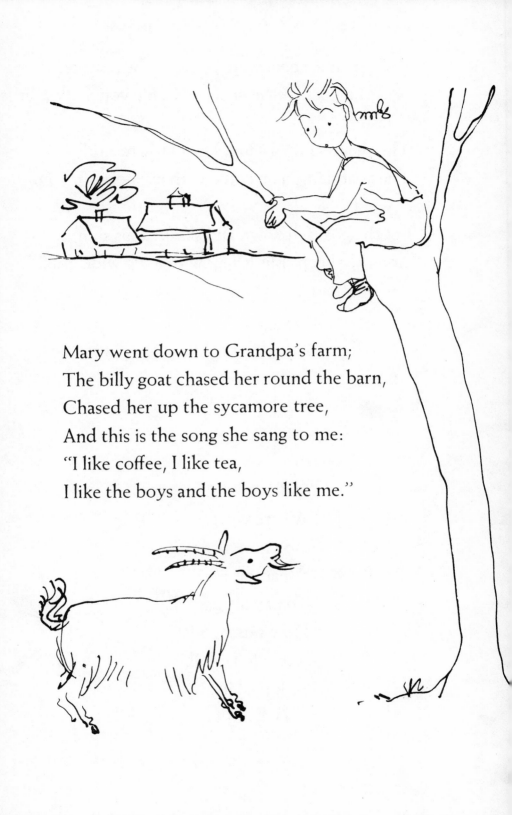

Mary went down to Grandpa's farm;
The billy goat chased her round the barn,
Chased her up the sycamore tree,
And this is the song she sang to me:
"I like coffee, I like tea,
I like the boys and the boys like me."

A sheep and a goat were going to the pasture.
Said the goat to the sheep, "Can't you walk a little
    faster?"
The sheep said, "I can't. I'm a little too full."
The goat said, "You could with my horns in your
    wool."
But the goat fell down and skinned his shin,
And the sheep split his lip with a big wide grin.

✳

"Hello, Bill."
"Where you going, Bill?"
"Downtown, Bill."
"What for, Bill?"
"To pay my gas bill."
"How much, Bill?"
"A ten dollar bill."
"So long, Bill."
[10]

A big turtle sat on the end of a log,
Watching a tadpole turn into a frog.

✳

Girls are dandy,
Made of candy—
That's what little girls are made of.
Boys are rotten,
Made of cotton—
That's what little boys are made of.

✳

Adam and Eve and Pinch-me
Went down to the river to bathe.
Adam and Eve got drown'ded,
Which one of the three was saved?

[11]

Early in the morning, let's go to the country.
See the little puff-puffs, all in a row.
Man in the engine pulls a little lever;
Choo-choo, whoo-whoo, off we go.

The elephant carries a great big trunk;
He never packs it with clothes;
It has no lock and it has no key,
But he takes it wherever he goes.

✳

I went down to my garden patch
To see if my old hen had hatched.
She'd hatched out her chickens and
    the peas were green;
She sat there a-pickin' on a tambourine.

✳

Me, myself, and I—
We went to the kitchen and ate a pie.
Then my mother she came in
And chased us out with a rolling pin.

I've got a rocket
In my pocket;
I cannot stop to play.
Away it goes!
I've burnt my toes.
It's Independence Day.

Said the monkey to the donkey,
"What'll you have to drink?"
Said the donkey to the monkey,
"I'd like a swig of ink."

✵

Possum pie is made of rye,
The possum is the meat.
It's rough enough and tough enough,
And more than we can eat.

✵

I love my wife and I love my baby,
I love my biscuits sopped in gravy.

✵

A little man of Teheran
Lived on the plain of Ispahan.
From Ispahan to Teheran,
To Teheran, tee hee!

Policeman, policeman, don't catch me!
Catch that boy behind a tree.
He took money, I took none;
Put him in the jailhouse, just for. fun.

Tom Teeple ate a steeple.
How could he do it, my good people?
I will tell you very plain:
Because it was made of sugar cane!

＊

Did you ever hear such a noise and clamor?
The hatchet's fighting with the hammer.

＊

I had a cow that gave such milk
I dressed her in the finest silk;
I fed her on the finest hay,
And milked her twenty times a day.

[18]

I'm a little Hindoo.
I do all I kindoo.
Where my pants and shirt don't meet
I make my little skindoo.

✿

A peanut sat on the railroad track,
His heart was all a-flutter;
Along came a train—the 9:15—
Toot, toot, peanut butter!

[19]

My father owns the butcher shop,
My mother cuts the meat,
And I'm the little hot dog
That runs around the street.

The old hen sat on turkey eggs,
And she hatched out little ones three.
Two were turkeys with slender legs,
And one was a bumble bee.
All the old hens said to each other,
"Mighty queer chickens! See?"

*

Once upon a time
A monkey drank some wine,
And then he danced a jig
On the street car line.

The street car broke,
The monkey choked,
And then he went to heaven
In a little tin boat.

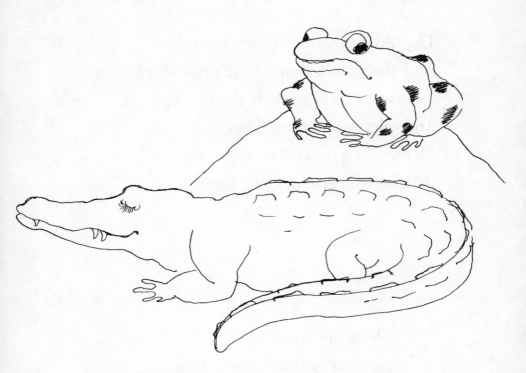

Oh, the bullfrog tried to court the alligator;
He hopped upon a log and offered her a tater.
Oh, the alligator grinned, and then she tried to blush.
And the bullfrog cried out, "Hush, oh hush!"

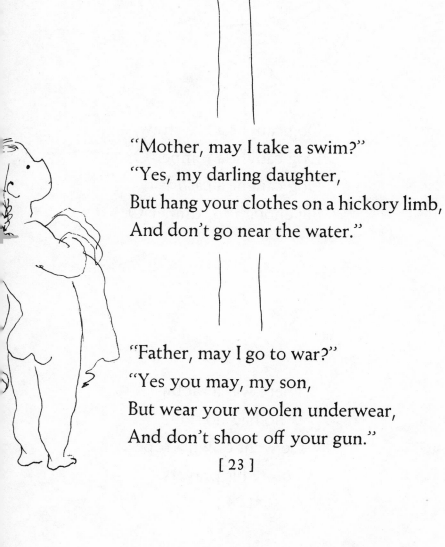

"Mother, may I take a swim?"
"Yes, my darling daughter,
But hang your clothes on a hickory limb,
And don't go near the water."

"Father, may I go to war?"
"Yes you may, my son,
But wear your woolen underwear,
And don't shoot off your gun."

[23]

Dog caught a rye straw,
Dog caught a minner-O,
Dog caught a catfish
Big enough for dinner-O.

✳

There was a rabbit
Who had no stairs;
He went down a rope
To say his prayers.

[24]

Jaybird a-sitting on a hickory limb;
He winked at me and I winked at him.
I picked up a rock and hit him on the chin.
Says he, "Young feller, don't you do that again!"

✳

Christopher Columbus!
What do you think of that?
A big fat lady
Sat upon my hat.

✳

I stood on the bridge at midnight,
When the clock was striking in town;
I stood on the bridge at midnight—
There was no place at all to sit down.

[25]

Wake up, Jacob,
Day's a-breakin'.
The beans are in the pot
And the hoecake's a-bakin'.

[26]

There was a little pig,
Who didn't grow big,
So they put him in a great big show.
He tumbled through a winder
And broke his little finger—
Now he can't play his old banjo!

✳

Five little squirrels sat up in a tree.
The first one said, "What do I see?"
The second one said, "A man with a gun."
The third one said, "Then we'd better run."
The fourth one said, "Let's hide in the shade."
The fifth one said, "I'm not afraid."
Then BANG went the gun, and how they did run.

✳

I had a little colt,
His name was Jack;
I put him in the barn,
But he jumped through the crack.

Joe, Joe, stumped his toe
On the way to Mexico.
On the way back he hurt his back,
Sliding on the railroad track.
When he got home he broke a bone,
Speaking on the telephone.

✻

Teddy on the railroad,
Picking up stones.
Along came an engine,
And broke Teddy's bones.
"Oh," said Teddy,
"That's no fair."
"Oh," said the engineer,
"I don't care."

✻

Way down yonder on the Piankatank,
Where the bullfrogs jump from bank to bank,
'Cause there's nothing else to do.

Jenny got so angry
She didn't know what to do.
She stuck her finger in her ear
And cracked it right in two.

Got a cornstalk fiddle
And a shoestring bow,
If you want to get to heaven,
You'll have to do just so.

＊

There was a little baby,
His name was Tiny Tim.
They put him in the bathtub
To teach him how to swim.
He drank up all the water,
He ate up all the soap,
And one day he choked
On a bubble in his throat.

＊

I know something I won't tell;
Three little monkeys in a peanut shell.
One can read and one can write,
And one can smoke a corncob pipe.

Old Dan Tucker went to town,

Ridin' a goat and leadin' a hound;

The hound gave a yelp and the goat gave a jump,

And old Dan Tucker landed on a stump.

[31]

Sam, Sam, the butcher man,
Washed his face in a frying pan,
Combed his hair with a wagon wheel,
And died with a toothache in his heel.

✦

Rin Tin Tin swallowed a pin,
He went to the doctor and the doctor wasn't in,
He knocked on the door and fell on the floor,
And that was the end of Rin Tin Tin.

✦

Smitty on the railroad, picking up sticks.
"Hurry up, Smitty! It's half-past six."
Smitty ran home, opened the door,
Kissed his mother, and fell on the floor.

Paddy O'Flynn had no breeches to wear,
So they bought him a sheepskin and made him a pair,
The woolly side out and the skinny side in—
They made very good breeches for Paddy O'Flynn.

Last night and the night before,
Twenty-five robbers knocked at the door.
Johnny got up to let them in
And hit them on the head with a rolling pin.

✳

Mary lost her coat,
Mary lost her hat,
Mary lost her fifty cents—
Now what do you think of that?

Mary *found* her coat,
Mary *found* her hat,
Mary *found* her fifty cents—
Now what do you think of *that*?

✳

Fat and Skinny had a race,
Ran around the pillow case;
Fat fell down and broke his face,
And Skinny won the race.

Every time I come to town,
They all start kickin' my dog around;
Makes no difference if he is a hound,
They got to stop kickin' my dog around.

[35]

I went to the animal fair;
The birds and the beasts were there;
The big baboon by the light of the moon
Was combing his auburn hair.

The monkey he got drunk
And sat on the elephant's trunk.
The elephant sneezed and fell on his knees,
And that was the end of the monkey-monk.

A horse and a flea and three blind mice
Sat on a curbstone shooting dice.
The horse he slipped and fell on the flea.
The flea said, "Whoops, there's a horse on me."

✳

Way down South in Grandma's lot,
The goose laid an egg, and the gander sot.
The goose looked this way, the gander looked yander,
Then the old gray goose started smiling at the gander.

✳

The raccoon's tail is ring-around,
The possum's tail is bare;
The rabbit has no tail at all,
But a great big bunch of hair.

✳

Raccoon up a persimmon tree,
Possum on the ground.
Possum said, "You big raccoon,
Shake those 'simmons down."

[37]

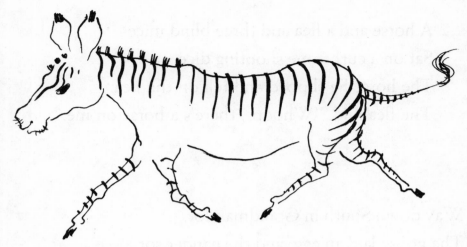

When the donkey saw the zebra
He began to switch his tail;
"Well I never!" said the donkey,
"There's a mule that's been to jail."

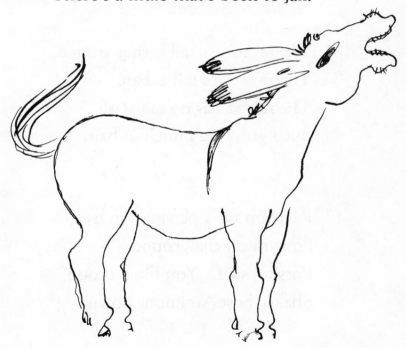

A lemon and a pickle knocked at the door;
They just came from the grocery store.
The lady went upstairs to get her gun,
You should have seen the lemon and the pickle run.

✲

Whoa, mule, whoa!
Can't you hear him holler?
Tie a knot in the end of his tail,
Or he'll jump through his collar.

✲

I eat my peas with honey;
I've done it all my life.
It makes the peas taste funny,
But it keeps them on the knife.

The boy stood on the burning deck,
Peeling potatoes by the peck.
When all but he had fled,
He looked around and said,
"Say, father, say,
Can I throw the peels away?"

＊

Down in the henhouse on my knees,
I thought I heard a chicken sneeze.
You ought to've seen me get away from there—
'Twas nothing but a rooster, saying his prayer.

＊

Charlie Chuck
Married a duck
Duck died
Charlie cried.

Mother dear,
I sadly fear
My appetite
Is always here.

[41]

I went down to the lily pond—
I heard an awful racket—
'Twas nothing but a bullfrog,
Pulling off his jacket.

✷

I once had a dog
That had no sense;
He ran round the house
And barked at the fence.

✷

One for the money,
Two for the show,
Three to make ready,
And four to go.

✷

Beef and bacon's out of season;
I want a knife to eat my peas on.

HIDE AND SEEK

Bushel of wheat, bushel of barley,
All not hid, holler "Charley."

Bushel of wheat, bushel of rye,
All not hid, holler "I."

Bushel of wheat, bushel of clover,
All not hid can't hide over.
All eyes open! Here I come.

*

It is a sin
To steal a pin;
It is a greater
To steal a potater.

Little Dick he was so quick
He tumbled over the timber;
He bent his bow to shoot a crow
And shot a cat in the winder.

✷

Johnny on the woodpile
Johnny on the fence
Johnny got a haircut
For fifteen cents.

✷

Matthew, Mark, Luke, and John,
Stole a pig and away they run;
The pig got loose and they stole a goose,
And all got thrown in the calaboose.

[44]

Matthew, Mark, Luke, and John—
I'm off my horse and I want to get on.
Open the gate and I'll be gone.

Oh say, kid!
What do you think I did?
I upset the go-cart
And out fell the kid.
The kid began to holler—
I grabbed him by the collar.
The collar broke loose,
And I got the deuce.

✳

"Fire, fire!"
Said Mrs. McGuire.
"Where, where?"
Said Mrs. Ware.
"Downtown!"
Said Mrs. Brown.
"Heaven save us!"
Said Mrs. Davis.

Oh, there's not much sense,
Sitting on a fence,
All by yourself in the moonlight.

✳

It's raining, it's pouring,
The little old man is snoring;
He went to bed with a bump on his head,
And didn't get up in the morning.

Bounce Ball

One, two, three, a-lary,
I spy Mistress Mary,
Sitting on a bumble-ary,
Eating a chocolate fairy.

*

One, two, three, a-lary,
My first name is Mary;
If you think it's necessary,
Find it in the dictionary.

*

One, two, three, four,
I spy Eleanor,
Sitting on the kitchen floor,
Eating a chocolate bar.

*

A lady in a boat
Wore a green petticoat
And her name is "Miss."

[51]

Baby in a highchair;
Who put her in?
Ma, Pa,
Whoops-a-la!

*

Down the Mississippi
Where the boats go PUSH,
Sat a little boy,
Eating mush.

*

One, two, three, a nation,
Doctor, doctor, there's a patient,
Waiting for an operation—
One, two, three, a nation.

*

A sailor went to sea
To see what he could see,
And all that he could see
Was sea, sea, sea.

Hippity hop to the barber shop
To buy a stick of candy;
One for me and one for you
And one for sister Mandy.

ALPHABET BALL

"A" my name is Anna,
My husband's name is Albert,
I come from Alaska,
And we sell apples.

"B" my name is Betty,
My husband's name is Bob,
I come from Boston,
And we sell bottles.

"C" my name is Clara,
My husband's name is Charles,
I come from China,
And we sell cats.

*And so forth—as long as the player can control
the ball and think up new names, places, and
articles to sell. The player turns a foot over the
ball on each "alphabet" word.*

COMPOSITION BALL

For each letter of the alphabet the player must recite a sentence in which exactly ten words begin with that letter. The player turns a foot over the ball on each of these words.

Anna and her adorable brother Alvin ate apples at their Aunt Alice's apartment.

❊

Betty Boop bought a big batch of bitter butter for her brother, Bobbie Boop.

❊

"Can Cousin Carol cook a good dinner for Cecil, who is a Captain in the army?" asked cute baby Caroline, as she ate a colored cookie.

Jump Rope

One, two, tie your shoe,
Three, four, shut the door,
Five, six, pick up sticks,
Seven, eight, lay them straight,
Nine, ten, a big fat hen,
Eleven, twelve, who will delve,
Thirteen, fourteen, girls a-courtin',
Fifteen, sixteen, girls a-kissin',
Seventeen, eighteen, girls a-waitin',
Nineteen, twenty, my stomach's empty.

❋

Miss, miss, little miss, miss;
When she misses, she misses like *this*.
Jumper steps on rope.

❋

I know a man—his name is Mister;
He knows a lady and her name is MISS!

❋

Jelly in the bowl,
Jelly in the bowl.
Wiggy waggy, wiggy waggy,
Jelly in the bowl.

The clock stands still
While the hands go around.
One o'clock, two o'clock,
Three o'clock . . .

One skipper is the clock—she merely jumps up and down. The other jumps clockwise around her.

✸

House to let,
Inquire within,
When MARY moves out
Let JANE move in.

✸

Mabel, Mabel, set the table,
Don't forget the salt and PEPPER!

At the word PEPPER the "enders" turn the rope very fast until the skipper misses.

✸

All in together,
How do you like the weather?
January, February, March,
April . . .

[60]

Two, four, six, eight,
Meet me at the garden gate.
If I'm late don't wait,
Two, four, six, eight.

*

Old Man Daisy,
You're driving me crazy,
Up the ladder, down the ladder,
One, two, three.
Pepper, salt, vinegar,
H, O, T !

*

Strawberry shortcake, cream on top;
Tell me the name of my sweetheart.
A, B, C, D . . . *Until jumper misses.*

*

Grace, Grace, dressed in lace,
Went upstairs to powder her face.
How many boxes did she use?
One, two, three . . .

Does he love me?
Yes, no, yes, no . . .

✳

Where will we get married?
Church, synagogue, house, barn,
Church . . .

✳

How many children will we have?
One, two, three, four . . .

✳

"Hello, hello, hello, sir,
Meet me at the grocer."
"No sir."
"Why sir?"
"Because I have a cold, sir."
"Where did you get your cold, sir?"
"At the North Pole, sir."
"What were you doing there, sir?"
"Shooting polar bear, sir."
"Let me hear you sneeze, sir."
"Kachoo, kachoo, kachoo, sir."

Apple on a stick
Makes me sick;
Gives me a stomach ache—
Two, four, six.

❈

I like coffee, I like tea,
I like the boys and the boys like me.
Tell your mother to hold her tongue,
For she did the same when she was young.
Tell your father to do the same,
For he was the one who changed her name.

❈

Here comes the bride
All dressed in white;
Here comes the fellow
All dressed in yellow.

❈

Gypsy, gypsy, please tell me.
What my husband's name will be.
A, B, C . . .
The letter on which the jumper misses is the initial of his name.

[63]

Indian, Indian, lived in a tent,
Indian, Indian, never paid rent.
She borrowed one, she borrowed two,
And passed the rope over to Y, O, U.

✿

Judge, judge, tell the judge,
Mamma has a new baby.
It's a boy, full of joy,
Papa's going crazy.
Wrap it up in tissue paper,
Send it down the elevator.
How many pounds did it weigh?
One, two, three . . .

Cinderella, dressed in yellow,
Went downtown to buy an umbrella.
On the way she met a fellow.
How many kisses did she receive?
One, two, three . . .

❋

Charlie Chaplin went to France
To teach the ladies how to dance.
Heel, toe, and around we go;
Salute to the captain,
Bow to the queen,
Turn your back
On the old submarine.

Little Sally Water,
Sitting in a saucer;
Rise, Sally, rise,
Wipe off your eyes.
Put your hand on your hip;
Don't let your backbone slip.
Turn to the East, Sally,
Turn to the West,
Turn to the one, Sally,
That you love the best.

✳

Charlie McCarthy sat on a pin.
How many inches did it go in?
One, two, three . . .

✳

Little Orphan Annie,
Sitting in the sun,
Had a piece of bologny,
And wouldn't give me none.
Take a bite, take a bite,
It's good for your appetite.

[66]

Sally over the water,
Sally over the sea,
Sally broke a milk bottle
And blamed it on me.
Sally told Ma,
Ma told Pa,
Sally got a scolding,
Ha, ha, ha.

✷

Popeye went down in the cellar
To drink some spinach juice.
How many gallons did he drink?
One, two, three . . .

✷

I should worry, I should care,
I should marry a millionaire;
He should die, I should cry—
Then I'd marry a richer guy.

There was a little girl
Dressed in blue;
She died last night
At half past two.
Did she go up?
Or did she go down?
Up, down, up, down ...

✻

I won't go to Macy's any more, more, more,
There's a big fat policeman at the door, door, door,
He grabs you by the collar,
And makes you pay a dollar.
I won't go to Macy's any more, more, more.

✻

I know a man named Michael Finnegan—
He wears whiskers on his chinnegan.
Along came a wind and blew them in again;
Poor old Michael Finnegan, begin again.

[68]

Mother, mother, mother, pin a rose on me.
Two young fellows are after me.
One is blind and the other can't see.
Mother, mother, mother, pin a rose on me.

✳

Dolly Dimple walks like this,
Dolly Dimple talks like this,
Dolly Dimple throws a kiss,
Dolly Dimple MISSES like this.

✳

Lady bird, lady bird, turn around,
Lady bird, lady bird, touch the ground.
Lady bird, lady bird, fly away home,
Lady bird, lady bird, you have gone.
Lady bird, lady bird, go upstairs,
Lady bird, lady bird, say your prayers.
Lady bird, lady bird, turn out the light,
Lady bird, lady bird, say Good night.
Teddy bear, teddy bear, point to the sky,
Teddy bear, teddy bear, show your glass eye.
Teddy bear, teddy bear, pull off your wig,
Teddy bear, teddy bear, dance a jig.

GEOGRAPHY JUMP ROPE

I took a trip around the world,
And this is where I went:

From America to Boston;
From Boston to Canada;
From Canada to Denver;
From Denver to England . . .
And so forth, as long as the skipper can think
up new place-names—or until she misses.

❊

My mother made a chocolate cake.
How many eggs did she take?
One, two, three . . .

❊

When Buster Brown was one,
He used to suck his thumb.
  Thumb me over, thumb me over,
  A, B, C.

When Buster Brown was two,
He used to buckle his shoe.
  Shoe me over, shoe me over,
  A, B, C.

[70]

When Buster Brown was three,
He used to scratch his knee.
   Knee me over, knee me over,
   A, B, C.

When Buster Brown was four,
He used to crumb the floor.
   Crumb me over, crumb me over,
   A, B, C.

When Buster Brown was five,
He used to catch the flies.
   Fly me over, fly me over,
   A, B, C.

When Buster Brown was six,
He used to pick up sticks.
   Stick me over, stick me over,
   A, B, C.

When Buster Brown was seven,
He went straight up to heaven.
   Heaven me over, heaven me over,
   A, B, C.

My old man number one,
He plays nick knock on the sun.
　　Nick knock, pollywog, jinga-zore,
　　My old man will play no more.

My old man number two,
He plays nick knock on a shoe.
　　Nick knock, pollywog, jinga-zore,
　　My old man will play no more.

My old man number three,
He plays nick knock on a tree.
　　Nick knock, pollywog, jinga-zore,
　　My old man will play no more.

My old man number four,
He plays nick knock on a door.
　　Nick knock, pollywog, jinga-zore,
　　My old man will play no more.

My old man number five,
He plays nick knock on a hive.
　　Nick knock, pollywog, jinga-zore,
　　My old man will play no more.

My old man number six,
He plays nick knock on a stick.
    Nick knock, pollywog, jinga-zore,
    My old man will play no more.

My old man number seven,
He plays nick knock on the heaven.
    Nick knock, pollywog, jinga-zore,
    My old man will play no more.

My old man number eight,
He plays nick knock on a gate.
    Nick knock, pollywog, jinga-zore,
    My old man will play no more.

My old man number nine,
He plays nick knock on a dime.
    Nick knock, pollywog, jinga-zore,
    My old man will play no more.

My old man number ten,
He plays nick knock when he can.
    Nick knock, pollywog, jinga-zore,
    My old man will play no more.

Tongue Twisters

A big baby buggy with rubber buggy bumpers.

✿

Toy boat, toy boat, toy boat.

✿

If he slipped should she slip?

✿

Black bug's blood, black bug's blood.

✿

Does your shirt shop stock short socks with spots?

✿

Double bubble gum bubbles double.

✿

Each sixth chick sat on a stick.

✿

Eat fresh fried fish free at the fish fry.

Three gray geese in the green grass grazing.

Six slim slick sycamore saplings.

*

Round and round the rugged rock the ragged rascal
ran.

*

An old scold sold a cold coal shovel.

*

Pardon me, madam, may I show you to a seat?

*

The cat ran over the roof with a lump of raw liver.

*

I bought a box of biscuits, a box of mixed biscuits,
and a biscuit-mixer.

*

She sells sea shells by the seashore.

If Peter Piper picked a peck of pickled peppers, a peck of pickled peppers Peter Piper picked. But if Peter Piper picked a peck of pickled peppers, where is the peck of pickled peppers Peter Piper picked?

Theophilus, the thistle sifter, while sifting a sifter full
of thistles, thrust three thousand thistles through the
thickness of his thumb.

*

Of all the saws I ever saw saw, I never saw a saw saw
like that saw saws.

*

A skunk sat on a stump. The stump thunk the skunk
stunk; the skunk thunk the stump stunk.

*

How much wood would a woodchuck chuck
If a woodchuck would chuck wood?
He would chuck what wood a woodchuck would
    chuck,
If a woodchuck would chuck wood.

Counting Out

Eenie, meenie, minie, mo,
Catch a tiger by the toe,
If he hollers let him go,
Eenie, meenie, minie, mo.

*

Eenie, meenie, minie, mo.
Catch a thief by the toe;
If he hollers make him pay
Fifty dollars every day.

[83]

One potato, two potato,
Three potato, four;
Five potato, six potato,
Seven potato, MORE.

*

Monkey, monkey, bottle of pop;
On which monkey do we stop?
One, two, three,
Out goes HE.

*

All around the butter dish,
One, two, three;
If you want a pretty girl,
Just pick ME.

[84]

My mother and your mother
   hanging out the clothes;
My mother hit your mother
   in the nose.
What color blood came out?
R, E, D, spells red.

✦

Ink, a-bink, a bottle of ink,
The cork fell out and you shine!

One, two, three, four, five,
I caught a fish alive.
Six, seven, eight, nine, ten,
I let him go again.

✷

Acka, bacca, soda cracka,
Acka, backa, boo.
If your father chews tobacca,
Out goes YOU.

Out goes the rat,
Out goes the cat,
Out goes the lady
With the big green hat.
Y, O, U, spells you;
O, U, T, spells out!

Riddles

Riddle me! riddle me! What is that:
Over your head and under your hat?
                              —Hair

✸

In Central Park I saw Uncle Jack,
Walking along with the world on his back.
                              —A terrapin

✸

Thirty-two white horses
On a red hill;
When you say, "Stop!"
They all stand still.
                              —Teeth

Round as a doughnut.
Busy as a bee,
Prettiest little thing
You ever did see.

—*A watch*

✳

A milk-white bird
Floats down through the air.
And never a tree
But he lights there.

—*Snow*

✳

Red and blue and delicate green;
The king can't catch it and neither can the queen.
Pull it in the room and you can catch it soon.
Answer this riddle by tomorrow at noon.

—*Rainbow*

I washed my hands in water
That never rained nor run;
I dried them with a towel
That was never wove nor spun.
—*Dew and Sun*

✳

What's in the church
But not the steeple?
The parson has it,
But not the people.
—*The letter "r"*

✳

Upon the hill there is a yellow house;
Inside the yellow house there is a cream house;
Inside the cream house there is a pink house;
And inside the pink house there's a lot of
little white babies.
—*Cantaloupe*

[93]

YYUR
YYUB
ICUR
YY 4 me.

—Too wise you are,
Too wise you be,
I see you are,
Too wise for me.

✷

Big at each end and little in the middle,
Digs up the dirt and sings like a fiddle.

—A dirt-dauber

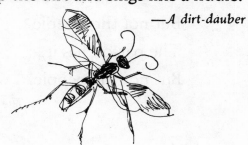

East, West, North, South,
A thousand teeth and no mouth.

—A saw

✷

Big at the bottom, little at the top;
A thing in the middle goes flippity-flop.

—A churn

Two-legs sat on Three-legs by Four-legs.

One leg knocked Two-legs off Three-legs;

Two-legs hit Four-legs with Three-legs.

> —*An old man sat down on a three-*
> *legged stool to milk his cow.*
> *When the cow kicked him, he*
> *hit her with the stool.*

✳

Railroad crossing, look out for the cars!

Can you spell that without any r's?

> —T-H-A-T

What has—
Four pusher-uppers,
Four puller-downers,
Two lookers,
Two hookers,
And a swishy-wishy?

—A cowsy-wowsy

The above is a 'foolish' variant of:
    Four diddle-diddle-danders
    Two stiff-stiff-standers
    Two lookers
    Two hookers
    And a swishabout.

✸

On the hill there is a mill,
Round the mill there is a walk,
Under the walk there is a key.

—Milwaukee

✸

As I went through a field of wheat,
I picked up something good to eat;
It had neither flesh nor bone,
But in twenty-one days it walked alone.

—An egg

Long, slim, slick fellow;
Pull a trigger and hear him bellow.

—*A gun*

*

House full, yard full,
You can't catch a spoonful.

—*Smoke*

*

Over on the hill there's a big red bull;
Feed him and feed him and he never gets full.

— *A threshing machine*

*

It has a head like a cat, feet like a cat,
A tail like a cat, but it isn't a cat.

—*A kitten*

Spelling Rhymes

A knife and a fork!
A bottle and a cork!
That's the way
To spell NEW YORK.

❉

A needle and a pin
Spell Cin, Cin, Cin.
A gnat and a fly
Spell CINCINNATI.

❉

Can you count?
Can you stand?
Can you con-stant-I?
Can you nople?
Can you pople?
Can you CONSTANTINOPLE?

Chicken in the car
And the car won't go.
That's the way to spell
CHICAGO!

✳

M, I, crooked letter, crooked letter, I,
Crooked letter, crooked letter, I,
Humpback, humpback, I.
MISSISSIPPI!

✳

H, U, uckle,
B, U, buckle,
H, U, uckle, Y,
H, U, uckle,
B, U, buckle,
HUCKLEBERRY PIE!

[102]

SPELL POTATOES

Put one-o
Put two-o's
Put three-o's
Put four-o's
Put five-o's
Put six-o's
Put seven-o's
POTATOES

B, U, hippity!
Double-L, croak and crunk!
F, R, splash
And O, G, sunk!
BULLFROG.

✻

Snoopy, snippin'
Snappin' urtle;
Fat and tickin'—
SNAPPIN' TURTLE!

✻

T, U, turkey, T, U, ti,
T, U, turkey, buzzard's eye;
T, U, turkey, T, U, ting,
T, U, turkey, buzzard's wing.

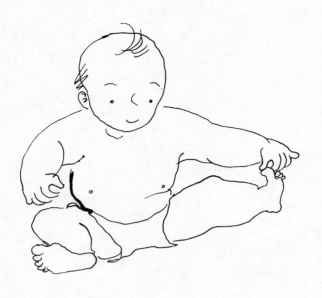

Fingers and Toes

Here is daddy's hayrake,
Here is mother's table,
Here is sister's looking glass,
And here is baby's cradle.

✷

There were two blackbirds, sitting on a hill,
One was named Jack, and the other named Jill.
Fly away, Jack; fly away, Jill!
Come again, Jack; come again, Jill!

This is the church,
This is the steeple;
Open the door
And see all the people.

✳

Here is the beehive. Where are the bees?
Hiding inside where nobody sees.
Now they are coming out. All are alive!
One! Two! Three! Four! Five!

✳

Brow-brinker,
Eye-winker,
Nose-nopper,
Mouth-eater,
Chin-chopper,
Chin-chopper,
Chin.

This little pig went to market,
This little pig stayed at home,
This little pig had roast beef,
This little pig had none,
This little pig cried, "Wee, wee,
    wee, I want some!"

KNEES

If you are an honest child,
As I think you be,
You'll neither smile nor giggle
When I tickle your knee.

✷

HEAD

Knock at the door,
Peep in,
Lift up the latch,
And walk in.

Banter

I know a secret!

✵

Smarty, smarty, smarty,
Thought you had a party.

✵

Sha-a-ame, sha-ame,
Everybody knows your na-ame.

✵

Rusty nail, went to jail,
For riding a pony without a tail.

[113]

Cry, baby, cry,
Stick your finger in your eye;
If your mother asks you why,
Tell her that you want some pie.

✳

NAMES

Girls

Anna banana
Played the piano;
The piano broke
And Anna choked.

✳

Jane, Jane,
The window pane.

✳

Margaret, Margaret, has big eyes,
Spread all over the skies.

[114]

Tit for tat,
Butter for fat;
If you kick my dog,
I'll kick your cat.

Sally bum-bally
Tee-ally go fally
Tee-legged, tie-legged
Bow-legged Sally.

*

Mary, Mary, don't say no,
Or into the closet you must go.

*

Rose, Rose,
Has big toes;
She carries them
Wherever she goes.

[115]

Burt, Burt, lost his shirt,
Had to hunt it in the dirt.

Bill, Bill, can't sit still,
Chased the billy goat over the hill.

Joe Blow!
What do you know?

*

Johnny bum-bonny
Tee-onny go fonny
Tee-legged tie-legged
Bow-legged Johnny.

*

One, two, three,
Johnny caught a flea!
Flea died, Johnny cried,
Tee, hee, hee.

*

Frank, Frank,
Turned the crank,
His mother came out,
And gave him a spank.

*

Jack, Jack,
Sat on a tack,
And went to bed
With a sore back.

Billy, Billy, strong and able,
Keep your elbows off the table,
This is not a horse's stable.

❋

Rich, Rich,
Fell in the ditch,
And didn't get out
Till half-past six.

❋

Ed, Ed, big head.

[118]

COLORS

Black, black, sit on a tack.

Brown, brown, you're a clown.

Green, green, you're a queen.

Purple, purple, you're a durple.

Red, red, stays in bed.

White, white, go fly a kite.

Yellow, yellow, wants a fellow.

Snow is white and coal is black.

If your pants are too loose, just pull in the slack.

Skinny, Skinny, run for your life!
Here comes Fatty with a butcher knife.

✻

Cowardy, cowardy, custard
Ate a barrel of mustard.

✻

My girl friend is a lulu,
I found her at the zoo-loo.

✻

Maggie Meek, the tail of a leek;
A plug of tobacco in every cheek.

✻

Two's company,
Three's a crowd,
Four on the sidewalk
Is not allowed.

[120]

Brass buttons, blue coat!
Couldn't catch a nanny goat.

All policemen have big feet!

There she goes! There she goes!
All dressed up in her Sunday clothes.

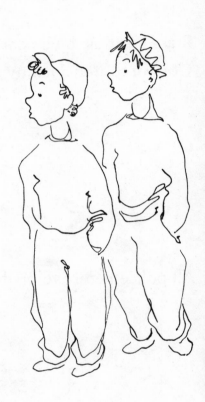

Ladies and gentlemen,
Take my advice:
Take off your coats
And slide on the ice.

[122]

Mary's mad
And I am glad,
And I know what will please her:
A bottle of wine
To make her shine,
And a nice little boy to squeeze her.

✳

Want a penny?
Haven't got any.

Want a nickel?
Buy a pickle.

Want a dime?
Some other time.

Want a quarter?
Jump in the water.

Want a dollar?
Sit on the roof and holler.

[123]

Stay mad, stay mad,
Be my little dishrag.

*

A BRAG

I'll tell you the truth!
Don't think I'm lying.
I have to run backwards
To keep from flying.

*

See this finger?
See this thumb?
See this fist?
You better run.

*

You're a poet.
You don't know it,
But your feet show it—
LONGFELLOW!

When they pass the pink ice cream,
Don't act as if you'd like to scream
Just turn your head the other way—
Act like you had it every day.

Eight and eight are sixteen,
Stick your nose in kerosene,
Wipe it off with ice cream.

Up the ladder,
Down the tree,
You're a bigger
Fool than me.

*

Open your mouth and shut your eyes;
I'll give you something to make you wise.

*

Teeter-totter, bread and water,
I'll be the son and you be the daughter,
I'll eat the bread and you drink the water.

*

Monkey see, monkey do,
Monkey speak—and so do you.

Tattle tale, tattle tale,
Hanging on a cow's tail.

✻

Good night
Sleep tight,
Don't let the bedbugs bite.

✻

Yes sir, no sir,
Maybe so, sir.

[127]

ANSWERS

Ask me no questions
And I'll tell you no lies.

＊

Sticks and stone may break my bones
But words can never hurt me.

＊

I'm rubber and you're glue.
What you say to me will bounce
back and stick to you.

Round and Round

STORY WITHOUT END

It was a dark and stormy night. Some Indians were sitting around the campfire when their chief rose and said, *"It was a dark and stormy night. Some Indians were sitting around the campfire when their chief rose and said,* 'IT WAS A DARK AND STORMY NIGHT. SOME IN-DIANS WERE SITTING AROUND THE CAMPFIRE WHEN. . . .' "

This can go on forever

The bear went over the mountain,
The bear went over the mountain,
The bear went over the mountain,
And what do you think he saw?

He saw another mountain,
He saw another mountain,
He saw another mountain,
And what do you think he did?

He climbed that other mountain,
He climbed that other mountain,
He climbed that other mountain,
And what do you think he saw?

He saw another mountain,
He saw . . .

MARCHING CHANT

Left! Right! I left my wife and twenty-four children alone in the kitchen without any gingerbread. Did I do right? Oh, by Jingo, I had a good job, but I left my wife and twenty-four children alone in the kitchen . . .

✵

THE GREATEST MAN ON EARTH

" 'E was the greatest man on earth."
"Who was?"
" 'E was."
"Who was 'e?"
" 'Arry 'Arrington."
"Who was 'Arry 'Arrington?"
" 'E was the greatest man on earth."
"Who was?"

And so on indefinitely

[133]

ENDLESS CHANT

"Who put the overalls in Mrs. Murphy's chowder?"
Nobody answered, so she said it all the louder:
"Who put the overalls in . . .?"

✷

ENDLESS RIDDLE

First speaker: Pete and Repeat were walking down
the street. Suddenly Pete went away.
Who was left?

Second speaker: Repeat.

First speaker: *Pete and Repeat were walking down the
street. Suddenly Pete went away.
Who was left?*

Second speaker: I said, Repeat.

First speaker: PETE AND
REPEAT WERE WALKING . .

A SOUTHERN CIRCULAR SAYING

A: You 'mind me of a man.
B: What man?

A: A man with the power.
B: What power?

A: Power to hoodoo.
B: Who do?

A: You do.
B: Do what?

A: 'Mind me of a man.
B: What man?   *Repeat from the beginning.*

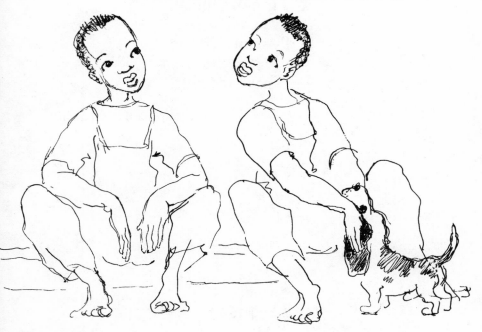

A: That's tough!

B: What's tough?

A: Life.

B: What's life?

A: A magazine.

B: Where do you get it?

A: Newsstand.

B: How much?

A: Fifteen cents.

B: I've only a dime.

A: That's tough!

Repeat from the beginning.

A: Don't go through that revolving door.

B: Why not?

A: My father is in it.

B: What's your father's name?

A: McGillacuddy.

B: Why, that's my name.

A: Father!

B: Son!!

Link Rhymes

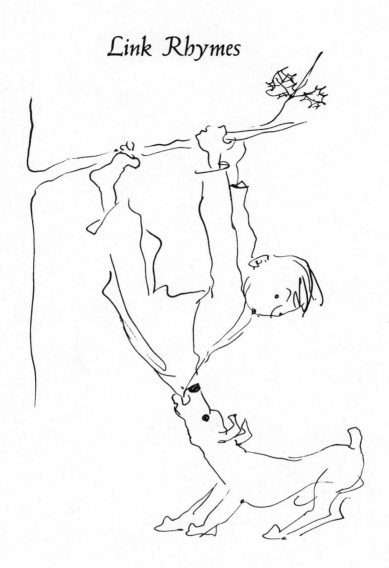

I went downtown
To see Mrs. Brown.
She gave me a nickel
To buy a pickle.
The pickle was sour,
She gave me a flower.
The flower was dead,
She gave me a thread.
The thread was thin,
She gave me a pin.
The pin was sharp,
She gave me a harp.
The harp began to sing
Minnie and a minnie and a ha ha ha.

I went down to the river
And I couldn't get across,
So I jumped on a mule—
I thought he was a horse.
The mule wouldn't pull,
So I traded him for a bull.
The bull wouldn't holler,
So I sold him for a dollar.
The dollar wouldn't pass,
So I threw it in the grass.
The grass wouldn't grow,
So I traded it for a hoe.
The hoe wouldn't dig,
So I traded it for a pig.
The pig wouldn't squeal,
So I traded it for a wheel.
The wheel wouldn't run,
So I traded it for a gun.
The gun wouldn't shoot,
So I traded it for a boot.

The boot wouldn't fit,
So I threw it in a pit,
And you fell in on it.

OLD OBADIAH

Old Obadiah jumped in the fire;
The fire was hot, so he jumped in a pot;
The pot was black, so he jumped in a crack;
The crack was high, so he jumped in the sky;
The sky was blue, so he jumped in a canoe;
The canoe was shallow, so he jumped in the tallow;
The tallow was soft, so he jumped in the loft;
The loft was rotten, so he jumped in the cotton;
The cotton was white, so he stayed there all night.

People, people, have you heard?
Papa's going to buy me a mocking bird.
If that mocking bird won't sing,
He's going to buy me a diamond ring.
If that diamond ring turns brass,
He's going to buy me a looking glass.
If that looking glass gets broke,
He's going to buy me a billy goat.
If that billy goat gets funny,
He's going to buy me a little pony.
If that pony runs away—
Ta, ra, ra, ra boom de-ay!

I had a little dog, his name was Ball;
When I'd give him a little, he wanted it all.

I had a little dog, his name was Trot;
He held up his tail, all tied in a knot.

I had a little dog, his name was Blue;
When I took him on the road, he almost flew.

I had a little dog, his name was Rover;
When he died, he died all over.

*

I had a little mule and his name was Jack;
I rode on his tail to save his back.

I had a little mule and his name was Jay;
I pulled his tail to hear him bray.

I had a little mule and he was very slick;
I pulled his tail to see him kick.

This little mule he kicked so high,
I thought that I would touch the sky.

I had a little mule, he was made of hay;
The first big wind that came blew him away.

THE GREEN GRASS GROWS ALL AROUND

In my backyard there is some ground,
The prettiest ground you ever did see,
And the green grass grows all around, around, around,
And the green grass grows all around.

And in that ground there is a hole,
The prettiest hole you ever did see,
Hole in the ground and the green grass grows all
  around, around, around,
And the green grass grows all around.

And in that hole there are some roots,
The prettiest roots you ever did see,
Roots in the hole in the ground and the green grass
  grows all around, around, around,
And the green grass grows all around.

And on those roots there is a tree,
The prettiest tree you ever did see,
Tree on the roots in the hole in the ground and the
  green grass grows all around, around, around,
And the green grass grows all around.

And on that tree there is a limb,
The prettiest limb you ever did see,
Limb on the tree on the roots in the hole in the
    ground and the green grass grows all around,
    around, around,
And the green grass grows all around.

And on that limb there is a branch,
The prettiest branch you ever did see,
Branch on the limb on the tree on the roots in the hole
    in the ground and the green grass grows all
    around, around, around,
And the green grass grows all around.

And on that branch there is a twig,
The prettiest twig you ever did see,
Twig on the branch on the limb on the tree on the
    roots in the hole in the ground and the green
    grass grows all around, around, around,
And the green grass grows all around.

And on that twig there is a nest,
The prettiest nest you ever did see,
Nest on the twig on the branch on the limb on the
tree on the roots in the hole in the ground and
the green grass grows all around, around, around,
And the green grass grows all around.

And in that nest there is an egg,
The prettiest egg you ever did see,
Egg in the nest on the twig on the branch on the limb
on the tree on the roots in the hole in the ground
and the green grass grows all around, around,
around,
And the green grass grows all around.

And on that egg there is a bird,
The prettiest bird you ever did see,
Bird on the egg in the nest on the twig on the branch
on the limb on the tree on the roots in the hole
in the ground and the green grass grows all around,
around, around,
And the green grass grows all around.

And on that bird there are some feathers,
The prettiest feathers you ever did see,
Feathers on the bird on the egg in the nest on the
twig on the branch on the limb on the tree on the
roots in the hole in the ground and the green grass
grows all around, around, around,
And the green grass grows all around.

✻

THERE'S A HOLE IN THE MIDDLE
OF THE SEA

There's a hole, there's a hole, there's a hole in the
middle of the sea.

There's a log in the hole in the middle of the sea.

There's a hole, there's a hole, there's a hole in the
middle of the sea.

There's a bump on the log in the hole in the middle
of the sea.

There's a hole, there's a hole, there's a hole in the
middle of the sea.

There's a frog on the bump on the log in the hole in the middle of the sea.

There's a hole, there's a hole, there's a hole in the middle of the sea.

There's a fly on the frog on the bump on the log in the hole in the middle of the sea.

There's a hole, there's a hole, there's a hole in the middle of the sea.

There's a wing on the fly on the frog on the bump on the log in the hole in the middle of the sea.

There's a hole, there's a hole, there's a hole in the middle of the sea.

There's a flea on the wing on the fly on the frog on the bump on the log in the hole in the middle of the sea.

There's a hole, there's a hole, there's a hole in the middle of the sea.

WHAT IS THIS HERE?

With my hands on my head, what is this here?
This is my THINKER, right over here.
That's what I learned in school.

With my hands on my head what is this here?
This is my I-SEE-YOU, right over here.
Thinker, I-see-you, hinky dinky do.
That's what I learned in school.

With my hands on my head, what is this here?
This is my SNEEZE-MAKER, right over here.
Thinker, I-see-you, sneeze-maker, hinky dinky do.
That's what I learned in school.

With my hands on my head, what is this here?
This is my SOUP STRAINER, right over here.
Thinker, I-see-you, sneeze-maker, soup strainer,
    hinky dinky do.
That's what I learned in school.

With my hands on neck what is this here?
This is my COLLAR HOLDER, right over here.
Thinker, I-see-you, sneeze-maker, soup strainer,

collar holder, hinky dinky do.
That's what I learned in school.

With my hands on my body, what is this here?
This is my BREAD BASKET right over here.
Thinker, I-see-you, sneeze-maker, soup strainer,
    collar holder, bread basket, hinky dinky do.
That's what I learned in school.

With my hands on my body, what is this here?
This is my BELT HOLDER, right over here.
Thinker, I-see-you, sneeze-maker, soup strainer,
    collar holder, bread basket, belt holder,
    hinky dinky do.
That's what I learned in school.

With my hands on my legs, what is this here?
This is my KNEE CAPPER, right over here.
Thinker, I-see-you, sneeze-maker, soup strainer,
    collar holder, bread basket, belt holder, knee
    capper, hinky dinky do.
That's what I learned in school.

With my hands on my feet, what is this here?
This is my SHOE HOLDER, right over here.
Thinker, I-see-you, sneeze-maker, soup strainer,
    collar holder, bread basket, belt holder, knee
    capper, shoe holder, hinky dinky do.
That's what I learned in school.

Autograph Album

Roses are red,
Violets are blue,
Sugar is sweet,
And so are you.

❋

Roses are red,
Violets are blue,
Grass is green,
And so are you.

❋

Roses are red,
Violets are blue,
What you need
Is a good shampoo.

❋

It tickles me,
It makes me laugh,
To think you want
My autograph.

[157]

May your life be bright and sunny,
And your husband fat and funny.

✹

If you love me as I love you,
No knife can cut our love in two.

✹

I love you little,
I love you big,
I love you like
A little pig.

✹

My love for you will never fail,
As long as pussy has a tail.

✹

Just as the vine
Grows round the stump,
You are my darling
Sugar lump.

[158]

Just as the mouse
Runs over the rafter,
You are the very one
I'm after.

*

You be the ice cream, I'll be the freezer;
You be the lemon and I'll be the squeezer.

*

Do you love me,
Or do you not?
You told me once,
But I forgot.

*

Pigs like mud,
Cows like squash!
I like you—
I do, by gosh.

[159]

I love you, I love you,
I love you so well;
If I had a peanut,
I'd give you the shell.

✻

When you stand upon the stump,
Think of me before you jump.

✻

When you see a monkey up a tree,
Pull his tail and think of me.

✻

If you think you are in love,
And still there is some question,
Don't worry much about it,
It may be indigestion.

✻

There are gold ships,
There are silver ships,
But there's no ship
Like friendship.

When you are courting,
It's honey and pie;
But when you get married,
It's "root, hog, or die."

*

When you get married
And live on a hill,
Send me a kiss
By the whippoorwill.

*

When you get married
And your wife has twins,
Just call on me
For safety pins.

*

When you get married
And your husband gets cross,
Pick up the broom
And say, "I'm boss!"

[161]

When on this page you look,
When on this page you frown,
Remember the one who spoiled it
By writing uʍop ǝpᴉsdn

✲

Like your books,
Like your toys,
But never, never,
Like the boys.

✲

My  4 U.

—My heart pants for you

✲

Read	see	that	me
up	will	I	like
and	you	like	you
down	and	you	if

When you get old
And cannot see,
Put on your specs
And think of me.

＊

U R
2 good
2 B
4 got 10.

You are
Too good
To be
Forgotten.

＊

Some write for pleasure,
Some write for fame,
But I write only
To sign my name.

[163]

I've thought and thought and thought in vain;
At last I think I'll sign my name.

❄

Can't think,
Brain numb;
Inspiration
Won't come.
Poor ink,
Bad pen;
That's all.
Amen.

Magic

You can't catch me,
You can't catch me,
My fingers are crossed
And you can't touch me.

*

Load of hay, load of hay,
Make a wish and turn away.

*

Star light, star bright,
First star I've seen tonight,
Wish I may, wish I might,
Have this wish I wish tonight.

*

I see the moon, the moon sees me,
The moon sees somebody I want to see.

[167]

See a pin and pick it up,
All day long you'll have good luck;
See a pin and let it lay,
You'll have bad luck all that day.

✴

I made you look, I made you look,
I made you buy a penny book.

First is worst,
Second's the same,
Last is best
In every game.

*

Rainbow at night, sailor's delight;
Rainbow at morning, sailors take warning.

Rain before seven,
Shine before eleven.

❉

A sunshiny shower
Won't last an hour.

❉

April showers
Bring May flowers.

❉

If a rooster crows when he goes to bed
He'll get up with rain on his head.

Step on a crack,
Break your mother's back.

＊

Step in a ditch,
Your mother's nose will itch.

＊

Step in the dirt,
You'll tear your father's shirt.

Whistling girls and crowing hens
Always come to some bad ends.

＊

Rain, rain, go away,
Come again some other day,
Little JOHNNY wants to play.

One for the cutworm,
One for the crow,
One for the blackbird,
And one to grow.

❋

Specks on the fingers,
Fortune lingers;
Specks on the thumbs,
Fortune comes.

❋

Wash and wipe together,
Live in peace forever.

❋

Laugh before you eat,
Cry before you sleep.

❋

Touch black, touch black!
You'll never get it back.

Drop a dishrag,
Someone coming to see you.

＊

Turn to the right,
You'll meet him tonight.

[173]

Finders keepers,
Losers weepers.

Ladybug, ladybug, fly away home,
Your house is on fire and your
        children will burn.

❋

Blue-eyed beauty,
Do your mother's duty;
Brown-eyed pickle pie,
Turn around and tell a lie.

[174]

If you stub your toe,
You're bound to meet your beau.

※

If you touch blue,
It's sure to come true.

※

Sneeze on Monday, sneeze for danger;
Sneeze on Tuesday, kiss a stranger;
Sneeze on Wednesday, get a letter;
Sneeze on Thursday, something better;
Sneeze on Friday, sneeze for sorrow;
Sneeze on Saturday, see your sweetheart tomorrow.
SNEEZE ON SUNDAY, YOU'LL HAVE COMPANY!

※

Hiccup, snick up,
Rise up, kick up,
Three swallers from a cup
Will end your hiccup.

[175]

One I love, two I love,
Three I love, I say.

Four I love with all my heart,
And five I cast away.

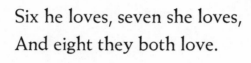

Six he loves, seven she loves,
And eight they both love.

Nine he comes, ten he tarries,
Eleven he courts, and twelve he marries.

Thirteen they quarrel, fourteen they part,
Fifteen he dies of a broken heart.

✳

Cut your nails on Monday, cut for health;
Cut them on Tuesday, cut for wealth;
Cut them on Wednesday, you'll get some news;
Cut them on Thursday, a new pair of shoes;
Cut them on Friday, cut for sorrow;
Cut them on Saturday, you'll take a trip tomorrow.

Whom shall I marry?
   Rich man, poor man,
   Beggar man, thief?
   Doctor, lawyer,
   Merchant, chief?

What shall I be married in?
   Silk,
   Satin,
   Calico,
   Cotton?

Who will be best man at my wedding?
   Tinker,
   Tailor,
   Cowboy,
   Sailor?

Where shall I live?
   Brick house,
   Log house,
   Frame house,
   Cabin?

How many children shall I have?
   One, two, three. . . .

Sound and Fury

A lady was chasing her boy round the room,
She was chasing her boy round the room.
And while she was chasing her boy round the room,
She was chasing her boy round the room.

❉

Our cat she crossed the road,
Because she crossed the road, sir.
The reason why she crossed the road
Was because she crossed the road, sir.

❉

Fuzzy Wuzzy was a bear;
Fuzzy Wuzzy had no hair.
Fuzzy Wuzzy wasn't fuzzy,
Was he?

❉

A fly and a flea flew up in a flue
Said the fly to the flea, "What shall we do?"
"Let's fly," said the flea.
"Let's flee," said the fly.
So they fluttered and flew up a flaw in the flue.

[181]

There's music in a hammer,
There's music in a nail,
There's music in a pussy cat,
When you step upon her tail.

✳

Where was Moses when the light went out?
Down in the cellar eating sauerkraut.

✳

Where was Moses when the light went out?
Under the bed with his feet sticking out.

✳

Where was Moses when the light went out?
Behind the door with his shirt tail out.

✳

Where was Moses when the light went out?
—In the dark.

If the lady of the house
Caught a mouse
In her blouse,
Would she holler?
Well, I guess she would!

*

Algy met a bear;
The bear was bulgy,
The bulge was Algy.

*

Did you eever, iver, over,
In your leef, life, loaf,
See the deevel, divel, dovel,
Kiss his weef, wife, woaf?

No, I neever, niver, nover,
In my leef, life, loaf,
Saw the deevel, divel, dovel,
Kiss his weef, wife, woaf.

If you and your folks like me and my folks
Like me and my folks like you and your folks,
Then me and my folks like you and your folks
Like you and your folks like me and my folks.

☀

Me no know,
Me no care,
Push a button
And go somewhere.

☀

One day a boy went walking,
And walked into a store.
He bought a pound of sausage meat,
And laid it on the floor.

The boy began to whistle—
He whistled up a tune,
And all the little sausages
Danced around the room.

[184]

I like myself, I think I'm grand,
I go to the movies to hold my hand.
I put my arms around my waist,
And when I get fresh I smack my face.

✻

Once an ant
Met a bat,
Said the bat
To the cat,
"Why the dog
Don't the elephant
Get the fish
Out of here?"

✻

One bright morning in the middle of the night
Two dead boys got up to fight.
Back to back they faced each other,
Drew their swords and shot each other.
A deaf policeman heard the noise
And came and killed those two dead boys.

[185]

I had a nickel and I walked around the block.
I walked right into a baker shop.
I took two doughnuts right out of the grease;
I handed the lady my five-cent piece.
She looked at the nickel and she looked at me,
And said, "This money's no good to me.
There's a hole in the nickel, and it goes right through."
Says I, "There's a hole in the doughnut, too."

Did you ever go fishing on a bright sunny day—
Sit on a fence and have the fence give way?
Slide off the fence and rip your pants,
And see the little fishes do the hootchy-kootchy dance?

✸

My mother bought a donkey—she thought it was a cow.
She sent me out to milk it, but I didn't know how.
The night was dark and I couldn't see,
And that old donkey took a bite out of me.

✸

It was midnight on the ocean,
Not a streetcar was in sight.
I walked into a drugstore
To try to get a light.
The man behind the counter
Was a woman old and gray,
Who used to peddle shoestrings
On the road to Mandalay.

Listen, my children, and you shall hear
Of the midnight ride of MARY dear:
First in a go-cart, then on a wheel,
And last of all in an automobile.

✳

Three little girls dressed all in white
Tried to fly to heaven on the tail of a kite.
The kite string broke and down they fell—
They didn't get to heaven but they didn't get well.

✳

I had a little brother,
No bigger than my thumb;
I put him in the coffee pot—
He rattled like a drum.

✳

Betty Boop,
Isn't she cute?
What she says is
Boop a doop-doop.

Mary had a little lamb,
She set it on the shelf;
And every time it wagged its tail,
It spanked its little self.

*

Mary had a little lamb,
Its coat was black as tar;
And everywhere that Mary went,
They thought it was a b'ar.

*

Mary had a little lamb,
Its coat was white as cotton;
And everywhere that Mary went,
That lamb it came a-trottin'.

*

Mary had a little lamb,
Its fleece as white as snow;
And everywhere that Mary went
—She took a bus.

Rockabye, baby, your cradle is hard;
Your pa picked it up in a junkman's backyard.

*

Humpty Dumpty sat on a wall,
Humpty Dumpty had a great fall.
All the king's horses and all the king's men
Had scrambled eggs.

*

Hickory, dickory, dock,
The mouse ran up the clock;
The clock struck one—
Time for lunch!

*

Rub a dub dub,
Three men in a tub:
The butcher, the baker,
The candlestick maker.
They all jumped over a hot potato.
Did they burn?
Did they burn?
No, no, no.

SCHOOL DAYS

April fool, go to school,
Tell the teacher you're a fool.

*

Tonight, tonight, the pillow fight,
Tomorrow's the end of school.
Break the dishes, break the chairs,
Trip the teachers on the stairs.

*

Up the river,
Down the lake,
Teacher's got
The stomach ache.

*

Four more days and we are free
From the school of misery.
No more pencils, no more books,
No more teacher's sassy looks.

*

Over the ocean
Tomorrow's promotion.

[191]

Over the bay
You'll get an "A."

*

Over the sea
"D" is for me.

✲

POLITICS

Sixty needles and sixty pins,
Sixty dirty Republikins

Sixty rats and sixty cats,
And sixty dirty Democrats.

✲

I bought a wooden whistle,
And it "wouldn' " whistle.
I bought a steel whistle,
And it "steel" wouldn' whistle.
I bought a tin whistle.
And "tin" it whistled.

Needles and pins, needles and pins,
When you get married your trouble begins.

＊

Do you carrot all for me?
My heart beets for you,
With your turnip nose
And your radish face.
You are a peach.
If we cantaloupe,
Lettuce marry;
Weed make a swell pear.

＊

Mississippi said to Missouri,
"If I put on my New Jersey
What will Delaware?"
Virginia said, "Alaska."

＊

Oh, you may drive a horse to water,
But a pencil must be lead.

[193]

BERTHA AND GERTIE

Boita and Goitie sat on de coib,
Reading de Woild and de Joinal.
Said Boita to Goitie, "Der's a woim in de doit."
Said Goitie to Boita, "De woim don't hoit,
"But it soitenly looks infoinal!"

✻

Oh, you never see a feather
In a tomcat's tail!

✻

Are you the guy
That told the guy
That I'm the guy
That gave the guy
The black eye?

No, I'm not the guy
That told the guy
That you're the guy
That gave the guy
The black eye!

[194]

Did he say I said you said she said that?
He said you said I said she said that!
Well, I didn't!

"Geat but not naudy,"
Med the sonkey,
Tainting his pail
Bly skue.

"Neat but not gaudy,"
Said the monkey,
Painting his tail
Sky blue.

❋

A great big molicepan
Saw a bittle lum,
Sitting on the sturbcone
Chewing gubble bum.

"Hi!" said the molicepan.
"Better simmie gome."
"Tot on your nintype!"
Said the bittle lum.

❋

In the valley in the vinter time,
Ven the vind blows round the vindow pane,
And the vimmen in the vaudeville
Ride velocipedes round the vestibule.

[196]

I went down to JOHNNY'S house;
Johnny had the measles.
This is the way the measles go:
Pop! go the measles.

*

Goodness gracious, save my soul!
Lead me to the sugar bowl;
If the sugar bowl is empty
Lead me to my mother's pantry.

*

Goodness gracious, save my soul!
Hang me on a hickory pole;
When the pole begins to bend
Slide me to the other end.

*

Now I lay me down to sleep,
A bag of peanuts at my feet.
If I should die before I wake,
Give them to my sister Kate.

[197]

I hear you say I say I say after every word I say I say.
I know I say I say after every word I say I say,
But it is not up to you to say I say I say after every word
I say I say.

✻

Through the teeth,
Past the gums,
Look out, stomach,
Here it comes!

✻

Lift the nozzle
To your muzzle,
And let it swizzle
Down your guzzle.

✻

Be's you got bugs?
Sure, I are—
Everybody do.

SMART ALEC ORATION

Ladles and jelly spoons:
I come before you
To stand behind you
And tell you something
I know nothing about.

Next Thursday,
Which is Good Friday,
There'll be a mothers' meeting
For fathers only.

Wear your best clothes
If you haven't any,
And if you can come
Please stay at home.

Admission free;
Pay at the door.
Take a seat
And sit on the floor.

It makes no difference where you sit;
The man in the gallery is sure to spit.

We thank you for your unkind attention.

The next number will be
The four corners of the round table.

﹡

If this book should chance to roam,
Box its ears and send it home.

﹡

A Word About This Book

A Word About This Book

A Rocket in My Pocket, which is published for the pleasure primarily of young Americans, should prove entertaining, as well as instructive, to their elders. It represents the spirit of the folklore of modern American children.

Here are brought together over four hundred of the rhymes, chants, game songs, tongue-twisters, and ear-teasers current in our time among youngsters living in many different regions of the United States. Every item of children's folklore printed here is a rhyme, or has some other arresting quality of rhythmical enchantment. The contents come from our largest cities, from remote backwoods areas, and from many smaller towns and villages that lie between; there will be no trouble in distinguishing bits that have a contemporary urban flavor from those reflecting life on our farms and in our little towns.

Many hundreds of children and grown-ups contributed directly, during the last ten years, to the making of this book. The editor collected much of the material himself through field work with children in New York City and in half a dozen rural communities in the midwest and the south. College students made another large contribution, for between 1940 and 1946, approximately two hundred Brooklyn College freshmen, under guidance, undertook short research projects in one branch or another of children's folklore, which brought in a vast amount of data from their own memories and from children whom they knew. Many adult friends also searched their memories to recollect folkloristic materials from childhoods spent earlier in this country. Books, professional folklore journals, and other printed sources were often used as leads in the quest for material, but in the end nothing was accepted for *A Rocket in My Pocket* for which the editor failed to find the sanction of an oral version.

Naturally, much more material was collected, and in many more categories, than could find its way into these pages, for the whole field of children's folklore is very large indeed. But the most delightful part of it, from the viewpoints of children themselves and of the editor, has gone in, that is the rhymed and other verbal rigmarole which trips off young tongues in games and banter, or which youngsters chant, sing, or simply "say," to entertain themselves and each other.

In this field of verbal nonsense American children are extremely inventive, and it is perhaps here that they have their greatest freedom for creative artistic expression. Through the ancient device of rhyme, and the still more ancient ones of furious alliteration and assonance, they have found a way to comment incisively, and often in very up-to-date fashion, upon the world of adults and upon other children. Their comments can be joyful, satirical, impudent, and even grim, but they are usually refreshing.

Some of the verses or songs included have long been familiar to English-speaking children everywhere, but a good many are printed here for the first time. The majority are "new" in the sense that American children have made them up either wholly or in part through transforming an old rhyme or saying to fit a new mood or situation.

Thus, this is more a book of inventions than of survivals. A generation ago, folklorists sometimes viewed innovations in the songs, legends, games, and other materials which they collected as corruptions of "original"—and even "superior"—versions. The modern folklorist, however, views change or invention as a vital process that accompanies the transmission and use of all folklore. He is more concerned with what people *do* with their folklore than with problems of origin and distribution.

Folklorists, educators, and child psychologists have become keenly aware of the importance of the folklore of children as a factor in social growth and development. Children live at the same time in two worlds—that of children and that of adults—and from the knowledge and activities of the latter world they are partly excluded. In modern urban life particularly, boys and girls tend to be gathered increasingly into rather narrow age-grades, each of which has its own folklore of games, practices, beliefs, social values, and special knowledge. This lore serves many social ends, including that of sheer entertainment. It plays an extremely large part in indoctrinating every child with the behavior patterns considered suitable for each stage of childhood, as well as with those of adult life.

The use that children make of the contents of this book is only partly suggested by the fourteen headings under which all the various items have been gathered. The classifications are useful but somewhat arbitrary, since a rhyme, if pleasant to the ear or tongue, has a way of showing up in new uses and contexts. The same rhymes often serve equally well for bouncing a ball or for jumping a rope, and a riddle-rhyme can be chanted "just for fun," without any concern for the answer. In the same way, a banter-rhyme can be shouted as a deadly insult or it may, like the familiar insult phrases of adults, be merely a friendly and ingratiating verbal token of affection.

Every youngster who reads *A Rocket in My Pocket* will find rhymes that he already knows—perhaps in a different form—but he will find many more which are unfamiliar to him yet are the favorites of his fellows in other parts of America. Parents, teachers, and other grown-ups who are interested in the mental life of children will see how greatly the content of children's folklore has changed since the days of Mother Goose. They will also find many clues toward understanding the enthusiasms, compulsions, and rebellions of today's crop of young Americans.

C. W.

Index

[207]

Brow-brinker, 108
Burt, Burt, lost his shirt, 116
Bushel of wheat, bushel of barley, 43
Bushel of wheat, bushel of clover, 43
Bushel of wheat, bushel of rye, 43

"C" my name is Clara, 54
Can Cousin Carol cook, 55
Can you count? 101
Can't think, 164
Charlie Chaplin went to France, 65
Charlie Chuck, 40
Charlie McCarthy sat on a pin, 66
Chick, chick, chatterman, 4
Chicken in the car, 102
Christopher Columbus! 25
Cinderella, dressed in yellow, 65
Cowardy, cowardy, custard, 120
Cry, baby, cry, 114
Cut your nails on Monday, 176

Did he say I said you said she said that? 195
Did you eever, iver, over, 183
Did you ever ever ever, 8
Did you ever go fishing on a bright sunny day, 187
Did you ever hear such a noise and clamor? 18
Do you carrot all for me?, 193
Do you love me, 159
Does he love me?, 62
Does your shirt shop, 77
Dog caught a rye straw, 24
Dolly Dimple walks like this, 69
Don't go through that revolving door, 137

Double bubble gum, 77
Down in the henhouse on my knees, 40
Down the Mississippi, 52
Drop a dishrag, 173

" 'E was the greatest man on earth," 133
Each sixth chick, 77
Early in the morning, let's go to the country, 13
East, West, North, South, 94
Eat fresh fried fish, 77
Ed, Ed, big head, 118
Eenie, meenie, minie, mo (1), 83
Eenie, meenie, minie, mo (2), 83
Eight and eight are sixteen, 125
Every time I come to town, 35

Far over the hills, a good way off, 3
Fat and Skinny had a race, 34
"Father, may I go to war?" 23
Finders keepers, 174
"Fire, fire!" 46
First is worst, 169
Five little squirrels sat up in a tree, 27
Four diddle-diddle-danders, 96
Four more days and we are free, 191
Frank, Frank, 117
Fuzzy Wuzzy was a bear, 181

"Geat but not naudy," 196
Girls are dandy, 11
Goodness gracious, save my soul! (1), 197

[208]